Thank you for purchasing this pr[...] it to contribute to your success in [...] questions of this practice exam h[...] close as possible to the type and difficulty of questions you will face on the CIPM exam, including a number of scenario questions.

The content of this practice exam is based on the latest exam blueprint to make sure that all domains are covered. In addition, the questions of the different domains have been mixed to disrupt the flow and train your brain to switch between domains.

There are no instructions on how to take this practice exam, because whether you use pen and paper or write in this document is completely up to you. However, flagging questions can be extremely useful. Train yourself in marking a question you don't immediately know the answer to in order to get back to it later (if you have time left), and you will greatly increase your chances of passing the exam.

There are 90 questions, for which you can take 2,5 hours. The available information regarding the percentage of questions you'll need to answer correctly is vague, but if you score about 80% you should be ready.

The first part of this document contains the practice exam, followed by the answer key. The second part contains the same questions, with the correct answer marked and some more information to lead you to the correct answer, as well as to show you how you could have been tricked into choosing the incorrect answer.

Good luck!

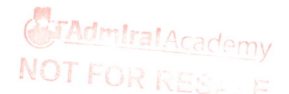

1. Which of the following is not a metric?
A. Data breaches
B. Return on investment
C. DDOS attacks
D. Minimize security threats

2. Which of the following is least likely a goal of a privacy program?
A. Legal compliance
B. Meeting customer expectations
C. Hiring a privacy officer or manager
D. Reducing risks

3. In which of the following ways can internal audit most likely help a privacy program?
A. Being in contact with the Data Protection Authority
B. Providing consultancy services
C. Reporting to the Chief Executive Officer
D. Approving privacy controls after testing them

4. What can be considered to be the essence of a privacy notice?
A. A layered explanation
B. A promise on handling
C. Icons properly displayed
D. Opt-in instead of opt-out

5. Which of the following is most true about privacy by design?
A. The option to reject cookies is privacy by design
B. Results, partly, in compliance with the General Data Protection Regulation
C. The automatic popup window asking to stop sending user analytics is privacy by design
D. Privacy by design is part of a privacy program

6. Which of the following is the best description of an accountable organization?
A. An organization that reprimands staff
B. An organization that states the Chief Executive Officer and Chief Financial Officer are responsible for privacy
C. An organization with the necessary policies and procedures
D. An organization that handles personal information correctly

7. Which step is likely not part of a privacy program with the goal to protect an organization's brand?
A. Prevent phishing using the company logo
B. Determine whether customers regard the company as transparent
C. See which regulations may not be complied with
D. Identify weaknesses in security

8. What is "the authority aims to safeguard the balance between the right to privacy and other rights"?
A. A goal statement
B. A Data Protection Authority guarantee
C. A mission or vision
D. The Data Protection Authority's legally required statement

Use this scenario for the following three questions:

A manufacturing company has placed computers all around the manufacturing area to help machine operators to relax during their lunch break and check their e-mails or social media. The company is doing so in an attempt to stop the machine operators from being distracted by their phones during their work and all the dangers that come with being distracted in a manufacturing area.

All the computers are connected to both the intranet and the internet. This allows an internal news bulletin and all policies and procedures to be displayed easily. There are regular updates, for example on family events, updates of procedures, bonus-related information and news on the employee of the month.

In addition to involving employees by sharing company news with them, all procedures are on the intranet. Anything from safe work practice guidelines to social media guidelines can be found on the intranet.

To use the computer, no login is needed. All computers are configured to be accessible to anyone, with ease. A downside of this is a shared hard-drive, and the older employees do not know that whatever they open on the computer is stored (temporarily).

9. In the scenario provided, where is the organization on the Privacy Maturity Model?
A. Defined.
B. Ad hoc
C. Repeatable
D. Managed

10. What is likely the biggest danger of a shared computer without user accounts?
A. It cannot be traced in case an illegal action takes place
B. There is a shift in responsibility regarding what a person does on social media
C. Employees can access each other's personal data
D. Every time someone uses the computer it constitutes a data breach

11. Given that the employees potentially see each other's data, a notice is visible on a piece of paper next to the computer. What can this be called?
A. A layered privacy notice
B. An opt-in notice
C. A just-in-time notice
D. An opt-out notice

12. How can you best describe metadata?
A. Information about data
B. The file types used
C. The time files are stored
D. The contact person for the data inventory

13. Which of the following is least likely or latest to implement a comprehensive privacy law?
A. The United Kingdom
B. Belgium
C. South Africa
D. The United States

14. A group of petrochemical companies set up guidelines and audit each other on its compliance and individual companies report their findings to the authorities if they find a law broken, what is this most likely?
A. Co-regulation
B. Self-regulation
C. Mutual auditing
D. Risk based auditing

15. How can a privacy standard be most appropriately described?
A. An approach to compliance
B. Getting a sponsor or champion
C. An approach to getting the organization to handle personal information correctly
D. Getting the right people in the right place

16. A company is subject to a certain law and assigned employees responsibility for compliance and developed Excel sheets for monitoring and reporting. What could this be called?
A. An auditable system
B. The compliance landscape
C. A comprehensive approach
D. A framework

17. Which type of organization has loose policies and managers that control small groups of employees?
A. Hybrid
B. Decentralized
C. Centralized
D. Diffused

18. When is a data protection Officer not necessarily required in the European Union?
A. For public authorities or bodies
B. When processing sensitive personal data on a large scale is the company's core activity
C. When a group of large office buildings and hospitals, including the persons inside, are systematically monitored
D. When processing the data of 10 000 employees

Use this scenario for the following three questions:

A popular music venue hosts an event at least twice a week. It sells a certain amount of tickets for each event, so the number of people that can enter is limited. At the events photographs are taken, which is indicated at the entrance of the venue (after the ticket check).

One day, an angry visitor shows up, demanding to speak to the manager. It turned out his wife saw him on the photos that were published on the internet, and he had told her that he was working overtime whilst instead he went to see his favorite band.

The manager assured the visitor that they have every right to take photos and publish them, as it is their venue and there was a sign before entering, so the visitor could have known and could have chosen to leave. In return the visitor responds that he did not see the sign, and when checking the sign he notices that there is no warning that the photos will be published on the internet.

19. When should the photo notice ideally have been provided?
A. After purchase of the ticket
B. Before the purchase of the ticket
C. Before publishing the photos online
D. Before the ticket is checked at the entrance so the customer has the choice to leave

20. In the European Union, if the processing of the photo was indeed illegal, what could the data subject have done?
A. Request access to the photo
B. Sue the company for damages
C. Get a refund
D. Divorce his wife for stalking

21. If the photographer is an external party, what would the photographer most likely be in this context?
A. A data subject
B. A data controller
C. A co-controller
D. A data processor

22. Which of the following is not an example of self-regulation?
A. DMA guidelines for ethical business practices
B. Binding Corporate Rules
C. Children's advertising review unit guidelines
D. Network Advertising Initiative Code of Conduct

23. When designing business processes, what is the most elaborate aspect to take into account?
A. Consent
B. Right to be forgotten
C. Processing on a legal processing criterion
D. Informing of automated decision making

24. Which of the following is not a country with its regulatory authority?
A. Indonesia - Minister of Communication and Informatics
B. South Korea - Minister of the Interior and Safety
C. Japan - Personal Information Protection Agency
D. New Zealand - Office of the Privacy Commissioner

25. What is the most likely reason for a data assessment?
A. To determine how the organization needs to handle the data
B. To figure out whether a Data Protection Officer is required
C. To assign responsibilities
D. To determine storage requirements

26. Which of the following is most likely not an element of a data inventory?
A. Information format
B. The requirement of contacting the Data Protection Authority in case of a data breach
C. Who receives the data
D. How information is used

27. Once a data inventory has finished, how would you most likely use the results?
A. Judge the Data Protection Officer's performance
B. Judge the Chief Information Security Officer's performance
C. Determine privacy priorities
D. Show the fault of a processor in case of a data breach

28. Why can multiple departments most likely be involved in a data inventory?
A. A sponsor is usually the Chief Executive Officer
B. Because the privacy manager is assigned to make the entire organization compliant
C. The sponsor is responsible for the entire organization
D. Because processes run through the entire organization

29. Which of the following is most likely to trigger the need to update the data inventory?
A. A new Data Protection Officer being hired
B. A new Chief Information Security Officer being hired
C. A change in the organization
D. A data breach

30. What is most likely the biggest benefit of buying an online data inventory software package?
A. A shift in responsibility for completeness
B. Updates with law changes
C. A data breach management module
D. Cloud backups

31. When developing a process for handling data breaches, which of the following is least important?
A. Timely reporting
B. Triggers for informing people
C. The involvement of the Chief Information Security Officer
D. Involvement of management

32. Which of the following is most likely assigned to the Internal Audit department?
A. Data Protection Impact Assessments
B. Privacy assessments
C. Privacy Impact Assessments
D. ISO 29134

33. When knowing there is a process that requires an in-depth risk assessment, which of the following is least advisable?
A. A Privacy Impact Assessment
B. A Data Protection Impact Assessment
C. An express Privacy Impact Assessment
D. An organization's own Privacy Risk Assessment template

34. Which of the following contains a set of guidelines for Privacy Impact Assessments?
A. ISO 14001
B. ISO 9001
C. ISO 29134
D. ISO 27001

35. Which of the following is most important for showing compliance with the General Data Protection Regulation?
A. ISO 27001
B. Privacy Impact Assessments
C. Privacy assessments
D. Data Protection Impact Assessments

36. What is not the goal of a security control?
A. Prevent
B. Detect
C. Administer
D. Correct

37. What would be the most likely reason to audit a vendor?
A. To compose a processing agreement
B. To take responsibility for outsourcing
C. To solve a data breach
D. To shift responsibility

38. When designing the process of obtaining consent, which of the following is least important?
A. To verify whether an alternative legal basis can be relied on
B. To design a way to properly record it
C. To figure out where in the process to ask for consent
D. To allow for the option of reversing the consent

39. What is the best description of a processor?
A. A cloud server
B. An organization acting only as instructed by another organization
C. An organization signing a transfer agreement
D. A part-data breach responsible

40. What is the biggest weakness of a Data Protection Impact Assessment?
A. The Data Protection Officer has to check
B. No Chief Information Security Officer input is legally required
C. Confidentiality, Integrity and Availability are not integrated
D. It is subjective

41. Which is most true about a privacy policy?
A. Required in the European Union
B. Contains templates
C. Policies are required to be approved by the Data Protection Officer
D. Provides guidance for decisions

42. Which of the following is least likely required of an organization?
A. Regulate
B. Verify
C. Define
D. Confirm

43. After or during a data breach, what will you most likely need the marketing department for?
A. Mapping processes
B. Sending out a mailing
C. Investigated the breach
D. Hide the trail

44. What is something communicated to people about privacy practices?
A. A mission statement
B. A privacy notice
C. A privacy strategy
D. Privacy policies and procedures

45. What is an acceptable use policy?
A. Specifies how people should behave on a network
B. A firewall setting
C. Part of the privacy program's output
D. Mandated as part of a code of ethics

46. Who is best to sign cloud computing agreements (if available)?
A. The Chief Information Security Officer
B. The Data Protection Officer or Privacy Officer
C. The Privacy Program Manager
D. The Chief Information Officer

47. Which of the following would most likely be considered a data subject?
A. Any individual or natural person
B. Any legal entity
C. A person linked to data
D. A patient visiting a small shop

48. If not responding quickly enough to a data subject's inquiry, which is not a likely consequence?
A. A missed legal deadline
B. A data breach
C. A complaint to the Data Protection Authority
D. A violation

49. Which privacy notice is most inappropriate under the General Data Protection Regulation?
A. A one-click 20 page PDF
B. An unreadable notice due to a website being offline
C. A notice that does not fit your screen
D. A notice aimed at children, thus oversimplifying the legal basis

50. What is an advantage of a layered privacy notice?
A. More complete
B. Receiving relevant information only
C. Everything in one document
D. Part of a website

51. What would be the least inappropriate use of a just-in-time notice?
A. Asking to access the location of your phone before starting your navigator
B. Asking you to write your return address on a package
C. At the time of an exam, informing you of the consequences of taking the exam
D. Your employer telling you the photos of the last company picnic are used on the company website

52. What is the most likely risk when deleting data too early?
A. Having de-identified data
B. Needing to ask for consent again
C. Not complying with a legal requirement
D. Not having the right encryption

53. Which of the following regulates the use of icons on websites and mobile screens?
A. The Data Protection Authority
B. The European Data Protection Supervisor
C. The Digital Advertising Alliance
D. The Privacy Ombudsman

54. What is the difference between express and implicit consent?
A. Opt-in versus opt-out
B. One always has a privacy notice
C. Implicit consent needs to be explicitly mentioned
D. There are no implications from express consent

55. Of the following, which is a big reason privacy laws needed to address privacy notices?
A. They have become lengthy and complex
B. They were not in machine-readable format
C. Consent was not required before
D. Too many unsolicited mails were sent

56. What is most important to do, if possible, when further processing personal data beyond the scope of collection?
A. Aggregate to an appropriate level
B. Use a copy in which names are removed
C. Inform data subjects
D. Update the privacy notice

57. When sending e-mails to data subjects, what can most likely cause an issue?
A. Mailbox size limitations
B. Cost of storage
C. A copy in the sent folder
D. Improper encryption

58. When setting up an automated mailing system, which is likely most important?
A. Delivering the privacy notice with the e-mail
B. Asking an opt-in prior to every e-mail
C. Proper retention periods of the e-mail
D. Ensuring the commercial message is not unsolicited

59. Which US state was the first to require a conspicuously posted privacy notice?
A. Delaware
B. California
C. New York
D. Minnesota

60. What is important to do before providing someone access to their data?
A. Setting up a retention scheme
B. Determining the legal basis
C. Seeing whether it fits the organizational workload
D. Verifying their identity

61. What will companies in the public eye relying on data most likely realize at some point?
A. A privacy program is required
B. Customer trust is needed
C. International data transfers are not necessary
D. Only with a privacy program can the company implement best practices

62. When someone wants his/her data corrected, what is the most likely point to pay attention to?
A. The organizational workload
B. The backlog of rectifications
C. Checking the new data for accuracy
D. The connection of data elements and locations

63. Why is it important to recognize an Article 15 General Data Protection Regulation request when someone sends a complaint to your organization?
A. Because of reputational damage
B. To remain having a legal basis for processing
C. Because of the legal deadline
D. To prevent a data breach

64. In the case of the data breach at Uber in 2016, how did Uber attempt to solve the situation?
A. Pay hackers
B. Increase security
C. Hire private investigators
D. Litigate

Use this scenario for the following three questions:

An internet reseller buys up cheap products and sells them for a slightly higher price. The company has a high turnover, and business is going well. There are only three employees working for the company, which is all that is needed as most is automatically shipped from a third party warehouse, with an online order that triggers an automated process.

Since the company is small, it does not standardize its work practices. Each employee has its own way of getting things done, and if needed they will ask the boss, who is generally in the same office and happy to assist.

One day, the server where all orders are stored is without password protection due to an accidental password reset. The cloud provider calls the company's boss to ask why they performed the reset, and after finding out that it was an accident, offers to check whether any external party has accessed the company's data in the hours it was freely accessible. This offer is refused, as the boss of the company regards the data not to be sensitive, as it only concerns customer orders.

65. In the scenario provided, where is the organization on the Privacy Maturity Model?
A. Ad hoc
B. Managed
C. Defined
D. Optimized

66. What should the company have done in light of the password reset?
A. No data breach took place, since accessing it would have been illegal, so no action is needed
B. The cloud provider is responsible in case of a data breach, so no action is needed
C. The company should have accepted the offer in order to determine whether a data breach took place
D. If a data processing agreement is in place, no action is needed

67. What would have been the case if an external person accessed the data?
A. It would have required immediate contact with the Data Protection Authority
B. It would likely have been a data breach
C. If the persons that accessed the data do not spread it, there is no issue
D. An audit should have been performed

68. Which of the following is a likely consequence of not knowing how and what you are processing?
A. Avoid liability of mishandling
B. Risk avoidance
C. Unaware of consequences of mishandling
D. Increase risk appetite

69. Development of your privacy awareness program can most likely be shared with which of the following?
A. The ethics and integrity department
B. The legal department
C. The management board
D. The audit department

70. Why do Chief Executive Officers not always give priority to privacy program implementation?
A. There is no risk of a fine
B. A secure cloud server is used in modern organizations
C. It does not generate revenue
D. The organization is small

71. Which of the following is the least common way to describe data about someone?
A. Private data
B. Personal data
C. Personal information
D. Personally identifiable information

72. Where was Privacy by Design most likely developed?
A. The European Union
B. The United States
C. The United Kingdom
D. Canada

73. A mobile phone application that will not function without an "unnecessary" connection to the internet at some point, is most likely not following which of the Privacy by Design principles?
A. Proactive, not reactive
B. Visibility and transparency
C. End-to-end security
D. Privacy as default

74. Which of the following is not Privacy by Design?
A. Being proactive
B. Embedded privacy controls
C. Demonstrating respect for users
D. Being reactive

75. When during the design of a process you consider making use of a third-party, which would be most exemplary of Privacy by Design?
A. Determining whether a third-party is needed
B. Using a well written contract
C. Ensuring only processors in safe countries are contracted
D. Involving the third party in the design

76. When password protection is too strict, which of the following is most likely negatively impacted?
A. Encryption
B. DDOS attacks
C. Availability
D. Integrity

77. If you are looking for guidance on the security management system implementation, which would you look?
A. ISO/IEC 2700
B. ISO 9001
C. ISO 14001
D. ISO/IEC 27003

78. When implementing a privacy program, what is important regarding access to files?
A. The Chief Information Security Officer should have access to all files
B. The Chief Information Security Officer determines who has access
C. Roles should determine access
D. Access is linked to individuals

79. Where would you most likely not find guidance on data breach reporting in the United States?
A. Comprehensive federal privacy law
B. State law
C. Industry-specific federal law
D. The General Data Protection Regulation

80. What would most likely help you get executives on your side regarding data breach prevention?
A. Showing the monetary impact of a data breach
B. Taking the General Data Protection Regulation as an example
C. Planning a meeting involving the Chief Information Security Officer
D. Indicating the statistical likelihood

81. Which of the following is the most common cause of a data breach?
A. System glitches
B. Failing firewalls
C. Simple encryption
D. Malicious actors

82. What is an informal readiness testing activity?
A. A policy evaluation
B. An incident response planning
C. Scenario testing
D. A tabletop exercise

83. What is likely the most important goal of metrics for an organization?
A. Legal compliance
B. Count data breaches
C. Inform the organization
D. Deter hackers

Use this scenario for the following three questions:

A clinic has just hired you as a privacy program manager. The clinic specializes in surgeries that reverse decisions taken by parents, such as circumcision, which patients wish to reverse due to disagreement with the decisions their parents took regarding their child's body. Your team consists of the privacy officer, which is close to the age of retirement and has been assigned the privacy officer job because nobody else wanted to do it, and the security officer who will start the same day as you.

On your first day you familiarize yourself with the staff and the procedures that are in place. You do so in an effort to determine the best approach towards compliance and optimal privacy practices. The task proves somewhat difficult, as it seems every doctor in the clinic maintains different procedures. The procedures are written down though, so that helps, but there is no data on compliance with the policies.

Besides the need to identify how the current situation needs to be changed in order to be compliant with the privacy legislation, the management board has purchased software that automatically sends data about the patients' treatment to their health insurance provider, saving the administrative staff a lot of work.

84. In the provided scenario, where is the organization on the Privacy Maturity Model?
A. Ad hoc
B. Managed
C. Optimized
D. Repeatable

85. If a patient named Achmet comes in for a reverse-circumcision, which of the following elements would least likely be considered sensitive personal data in the European Union?
A. Bank account and insurance number
B. The likelihood of a certain religion
C. The information of a venereal disease
D. Any complications after the surgery

86. Since it is unclear whether the procedures that are already in place are effective and/or followed, what is the best approach to find out?
A. Management evaluation
B. The verdict of the Chief Information Security Officer
C. The use of metrics
D. Composing Binding Corporate Rules

87. What could be a possible advantage of implementing a market leader's privacy metrics software as opposed to your own?
A. Automatic registration
B. High security
C. Benchmarking
D. Lower likelihood of a data breach

88. What right is granted under the Federal Credit Reporting Act?
A. The right to be forgotten
B. No adverse decisions to be made
C. Blocking credit reports from being used
D. Access to all information a consumer reporting agency has on them

89. To whom/what should the Data Protection Officer report in an organization in the European Union?
A. The Chief Information Security Officer
B. The Chief Financial Officer
C. The Chief Information Officer
D. The Chief Executive Officer

90. What is a regular, ad hoc or on demand process of checking control elements?
A. Control testing
B. An audit
C. A firewall test run
D. Privacy metrics

Correct answers:
1D, 2C, 3B, 4B, 5B, 6C, 7A, 8C, 9D, 10C, 11C, 12A, 13D, 14B, 15C, 16D, 17B, 18D, 19B, 20B, 21D, 22B, 23A, 24C, 25A, 26B, 27C, 28D, 29C, 30B, 31C, 32B, 33C, 34C, 35D, 36C, 37B, 38A, 39B, 40D, 41D, 42A, 43B, 44B, 45A, 46D, 47C, 48B, 49A, 50B, 51A, 52C, 53C, 54A, 55A, 56A, 57D, 58D, 59B, 60D, 61B, 62D, 63C, 64A, 65A, 66C, 67B, 68C, 69A, 70C, 71A, 72D, 73C, 74D, 75A, 76C, 77D, 78C, 79A, 80A, 81D, 82D, 83C, 84D, 85A, 86C, 87C, 88D, 89D, 90B

Explanations:
1. Which of the following is not a metric?
A. Data breaches
B. Return on investment
C. DDOS attacks
D. Minimize security threats (correct)
More information:
"Minimizing security threats" is a goal and not a metric. "Security threats" could be a metric, since it can be measured how many security threats there are. A and C can be measured, and B may not seem measurable but is a common metric.

2. Which of the following is least likely a goal of a privacy program?
A. Legal compliance
B. Meeting customer expectations
C. Hiring a privacy officer or manager (correct)
D. Reducing risks
More information:
The hiring of a privacy officer or manager is not likely a goal of the privacy program. There should already be a privacy officer or manager before the program starts, or perhaps the organizations can do without a privacy officer or manager. The other options are more likely.

3. In which of the following ways can internal audit most likely help a privacy program?
A. Being in contact with the Data Protection Authority
B. Providing consultancy services (correct)
C. Reporting to the Chief Executive Officer
D. Approving privacy controls after testing them
More information:
The internal audit department cannot perform any tasks that assume responsibility for any decisions taken, so nothing can be approved and no contact on behalf of the organization is to be had outside the organization. It can report to the Chief Executive Officer, but this does not help the privacy program. Consultancy services are a common activity for the internal audit department, so option B is the correct answer.

4. What can be considered to be the essence of a privacy notice?
A. A layered explanation
B. A promise on handling (correct)
C. Icons properly displayed
D. Opt-in instead of opt-out
More information:
In a privacy notice it is explained which data is collected and what is done with that data and why. So it is a promise of an organization towards the data subject on how its data will be handled. Option A is only applicable to layered privacy notices, and not the essence. Option C and D are not privacy notices, but part of a privacy notice, and also not the essence.

5. Which of the following is most true about privacy by design?
A. The option to reject cookies is privacy by design
B. Results, partly, in compliance with the General Data Protection Regulation (correct)
C. The automatic popup window asking to stop sending user analytics is privacy by design
D. Privacy by design is part of a privacy program
More information:
The General Data Protection Regulation specifies in Article 25 that Data Protection by design and default is required. Hence, privacy by design would result in compliance with this article and therefore with part of the General Data Protection Regulation. Option B is the correct answer. A and C are reactive and could have been preventatively done. Option D is not necessarily the case nor is it required.

6. Which of the following is the best description of an accountable organization?
A. An organization that reprimands staff
B. An organization that states the Chief Executive Officer and Chief Financial Officer are responsible for privacy
C. An organization with the necessary policies and procedures (correct)
D. An organization that handles personal information correctly
More information:
Procedures and policies likely indicate who is responsible for what, meaning the organization takes accountability for the practices of the organization. Option C is the correct answer. You can handle personal information correctly without being accountable, so option D is incorrect. Option A does not mean accountability, and option B does not make the organization itself accountable. There is no 100% correct answer here, just a most likely answer. Questions like this will be on the exam.

7. Which step is likely not part of a privacy program with the goal to protect an organization's brand?
A. Prevent phishing using the company logo (correct)
B. Determine whether customers regard the company as transparent
C. See which regulations may not be complied with
D. Identify weaknesses in security
More information:
What people do outside the organization cannot be controlled, hence it is not likely that a privacy program has the goal to prevent criminals from using their organization's logo. Option A is the correct answer. The other options could be goals of the privacy program contributing to the protection of an organization's brand (increased perception of privacy/security practices leads to a more trustworthy brand).

8. What is "the authority aims to safeguard the balance between the right to privacy and other rights"?
A. A goal statement
B. A Data Protection Authority guarantee
C. A mission or vision (correct)
D. The Data Protection Authority's legally required statement
More information:
In your study material you will find this in the part on mission and vision. The statement is not a goal, guarantee or required statement, hence option C is the correct answer.

Use this scenario for the following three questions:

A manufacturing company has placed computers all around the manufacturing area to help machine operators to relax during their lunch break and check their e-mails or social media. The company is doing so in an attempt to stop the machine operators from being distracted by their phones during their work and all the dangers that come with being distracted in a manufacturing area.

All the computers are connected to both the intranet and the internet. This allows an internal news bulletin and all policies and procedures to be displayed easily. There are regular updates, for example on family events, updates of procedures, bonus-related information and news on the employee of the month.

In addition to involving employees by sharing company news with them, all procedures are on the intranet. Anything from safe work practice guidelines to social media guidelines can be found on the intranet.

To use the computer, no login is needed. All computers are configured to be accessible to anyone, with ease. A downside of this is a shared hard-drive, and the older employees do not know that whatever they open on the computer is stored (temporarily).

9. In the scenario provided, where is the organization on the Privacy Maturity Model?
A. Defined.
B. Ad hoc
C. Repeatable
D. Managed (correct)
More information:
Since it is clear from the scenario that the procedures are updated and these updates are communicated, the procedures are likely also reviewed. This indicates that the organization is at level Managed.

10. What is likely the biggest danger of a shared computer without user accounts?
A. It cannot be traced in case an illegal action takes place
B. There is a shift in responsibility regarding what a person does on social media
C. Employees can access each other's personal data (correct)
D. Every time someone uses the computer it constitutes a data breach
More information:
Cookies, stored logins, downloaded files, etcetera, all can cause things to be revealed about the person that used the computer before, hence option C is the correct answer. Option A may seem correct, but the time of the illegal action together with CCTV or other information can lead to tracing the actions back to a single person.

11. Given that the employees potentially see each other's data, a notice is visible on a piece of paper next to the computer. What can this be called?
A. A layered privacy notice
B. An opt-in notice
C. A just-in-time notice (correct)
D. An opt-out notice
More information:
This can be considered a just-in-time notice, as it is provided immediately before it becomes relevant. Option A is the correct answer. There is no opt-out or opt-in involved, so B and D are incorrect. A could be the case, but not necessarily, hence is less correct than option C.

12. How can you best describe metadata?
A. Information about data (correct)
B. The file types used
C. The time files are stored
D. The contact person for the data inventory
More information:
Metadata is data about data, so option A is the best and most complete description amongst the options provided.

13. Which of the following is least likely or latest to implement a comprehensive privacy law?
A. The United Kingdom
B. Belgium
C. South Africa
D. The United States (correct)
More information:
In the United States there are no comprehensive privacy laws. See the chapter in your study materials that discuss comprehensive and other types of legislation. Option D is the correct answer. South Africa has the Protection of Personal Information Act, Belgium the General Data Protection Regulation and the United Kingdom (at least before BREXIT) the General Data Protection Regulation.

14. A group of petrochemical companies set up guidelines and audit each other on its compliance and individual companies report their findings to the authorities if they find a law broken, what is this most likely?
A. Co-regulation
B. Self-regulation (correct)
C. Mutual auditing
D. Risk based auditing
More information:
Regardless of any reporting of violations of other laws, the companies setting up guidelines for their industries is the companies self-regulating. Option B is the correct answer.

15. How can a privacy standard be most appropriately described?
A. An approach to compliance
B. Getting a sponsor or champion
C. An approach to getting the organization to handle personal information correctly (correct)
D. Getting the right people in the right place
More information:
Option C is the most complete answer. Option A is technically correct, but there is generally more to a privacy standard than compliance. Whenever you encounter a question where more answers seem correct, and you are sure that technically they are correct, try to figure out which one best addresses the answer in terms of completeness.

16. A company is subject to a certain law and assigned employees responsibility for compliance and developed Excel sheets for monitoring and reporting. What could this be called?
A. An auditable system
B. The compliance landscape
C. A comprehensive approach
D. A framework (correct)
More information:
A framework can refer to processes, tools, templates and laws. See your study material. Assigning responsibility is usually captured in procedures, and in addition with the Excel sheets for monitoring and reporting (tools), this fits the description of framework better than the other options. Hence, D is the correct answer.

17. Which type of organization has loose policies and managers that control small groups of employees?
A. Hybrid
B. Decentralized (correct)
C. Centralized
D. Diffused
More information:
A decentralized organization has control spread throughout the organization, and managers have smaller groups of employees. Option B is the correct answer.

18. When is a data protection Officer not necessarily required in the European Union?
A. For public authorities or bodies
B. When processing sensitive personal data on a large scale is the company's core activity
C. When a group of large office buildings and hospitals, including the persons inside, are systematically monitored
D. When processing the data of 10 000 employees (correct)
More information:
Large groups of data subjects is not mentioned in Article 37 of the General Data Protection Regulation. The other options are. Option D is the correct answer. Option C is phrased a bit more specific, but describes systematic monitoring on a large scale, to which Article 37 (1) (b) applies. Do not be mislead by how specific answers are phrased, and think about what the meaning is.

Use this scenario for the following three questions:

A popular music venue hosts an event at least twice a week. It sells a certain amount of tickets for each event, so the number of people that can enter is limited. At the events photographs are taken, which is indicated at the entrance of the venue (after the ticket check).

One day, an angry visitor shows up, demanding to speak to the manager. It turned out his wife saw him on the photos that were published on the internet, and he had told her that he was working overtime whilst instead he went to see his favorite band.

The manager assured the visitor that they have every right to take photos and publish them, as it is their venue and there was a sign before entering, so the visitor could have known and could have chosen to leave. In return the visitor responds that he did not see the sign, and when checking the sign he notices that there is no warning that the photos will be published on the internet.

19. When should the photo notice ideally have been provided?
A. After purchase of the ticket
B. Before the purchase of the ticket (correct)
C. Before publishing the photos online
D. Before the ticket is checked at the entrance so the customer has the choice to leave

More information:
If the privacy notice was provided before the purchase of the ticket, the person could have decided not to buy the ticket if he did not want photos to be taken of him. This would then have the least negative impact of the options provided, because if the privacy notice would be provided at any point after, the person would have the barrier of not visiting a concert he paid for and anticipated on going to.

20. In the European Union, if the processing of the photo was indeed illegal, what could the data subject have done?
A. Request access to the photo
B. Sue the company for damages (correct)
C. Get a refund
D. Divorce his wife for stalking

More information:
Article 82 of the General Data Protection Regulation allows for data subjects to receive compensation for any material or immaterial damages due to an infringement. Option B is the correct answer. Option A is also correct, in a way, but the photo is online and an organization does not have to provide anything the data subject already has access to.

21. If the photographer is an external party, what would the photographer most likely be in this context?
A. A data subject
B. A data controller
C. A co-controller
D. A data processor (correct)
More information:
If a photographer takes photos on the request/instruction of the music venue, then it is a data processor and the music venue is the data controller. Option D is the correct answer.

22. Which of the following is not an example of self-regulation?
A. DMA guidelines for ethical business practices
B. Binding Corporate Rules (correct)
C. Children's advertising review unit guidelines
D. Network Advertising Initiative Code of Conduct
More information:
Binding Corporate Rules are not required to regulate, they are merely internal rules towards compliance with the General Data Protection Regulation for international companies that transfer data between countries (outside of the European Union). Option B is the correct answer.

23. When designing business processes, what is the most elaborate aspect to take into account?
A. Consent (correct)
B. Right to be forgotten
C. Processing on a legal processing criterion
D. Informing of automated decision making
More information:
Consent is the most complicated of the options provided. It needs to be retractable and it needs to be registered. This has implications for the rest of the process. The others are less elaborate. Option A is the correct answer.

24. Which of the following is not a country with its regulatory authority?
A. Indonesia - Minister of Communication and Informatics
B. South Korea - Minister of the Interior and Safety
C. Japan - Personal Information Protection Agency (correct)
D. New Zealand - Office of the Privacy Commissioner
More information:
Option C contains a mistake, it should be Commission instead of Agency. This is an incredibly annoying question, which you will probably have to guess. The reason it is left in this practice exam is that there will be questions on the actual exam that are there to be tested, for which you will also have to guess. So, to more accurately reflect your score, there are some "impossible" questions in this practice exam which are meant to only be guessed.

25. What is the most likely reason for a data assessment?
A. To determine how the organization needs to handle the data (correct)
B. To figure out whether a Data Protection Officer is required
C. To assign responsibilities
D. To determine storage requirements
More information:
Option A and B are correct, but option A is more complete and hence the correct answer. A data assessment is an assessment to determine where you stand and where you need to go with regards to the handling of personal information/data.

26. Which of the following is most likely not an element of a data inventory?
A. Information format
B. The requirement of contacting the Data Protection Authority in case of a data breach (correct)
C. Who receives the data
D. How information is used
More information:
It is not legally required to add the requirement of contacting the Data Protection Authority in your data inventory. There should be a procedure for handling data breaches, where this topic is likely handled, but there is no obvious benefit to adding it as an element to the data inventory. Option B is the correct answer.

27. Once a data inventory has finished, how would you most likely use the results?
A. Judge the Data Protection Officer's performance
B. Judge the Chief Information Security Officer's performance
C. Determine privacy priorities (correct)
D. Show the fault of a processor in case of a data breach
More information:
When you know what data you have, why you are processing it, what the retention periods are and which security level it requires, you will likely also have identified the gaps between the actual and the desired situation. Based on this you can take actions and set the priorities of these (and possible previously unfinished) actions. Option C is the correct answer.

28. Why can multiple departments most likely be involved in a data inventory?
A. A sponsor is usually the Chief Executive Officer
B. Because the privacy manager is assigned to make the entire organization compliant
C. The sponsor is responsible for the entire organization
D. Because processes run through the entire organization (correct)
More information:
Processes run through an entire organization. The output of the processing of one department is likely the input for the processing of another department. Therefore, it is likely that every organization has processes that run through the entire organization, which needs to be reflected in the data inventory. Option D is the correct answer.

29. Which of the following is most likely to trigger the need to update the data inventory?
A. A new Data Protection Officer being hired
B. A new Chief Information Security Officer being hired
C. A change in the organization (correct)
D. A data breach
More information:
When there is a change in the organization, and this affects a process, this changes the use of personal data and should trigger a review and update of the data inventory. Maintaining a data inventory is a continuous process, and many organizational changes can trigger a change in the way of processing personal data and therefore the need to review and update the data inventory. Option C is the correct answer.

30. What is most likely the biggest benefit of buying an online data inventory software package?
A. A shift in responsibility for completeness
B. Updates with law changes (correct)
C. A data breach management module
D. Cloud backups
More information:
Laws and case law create change every now and then, which can affect what is legally required to be in the data inventory and in which depth (think of whether you consider the hiring process as one entry, or do you split it in application, selection, etcetera). A supplier is likely to update his software, which can save an organization a lot of effort. Option B is the correct answer.

31. When developing a process for handling data breaches, which of the following is least important?
A. Timely reporting
B. Triggers for informing people
C. The involvement of the Chief Information Security Officer (correct)
D. Involvement of management
More information:
Although the involvement of the Chief Information Security Officer can be important, it is less important than the other options provided. Management needs to take decisions, it needs to be clear which people need to be involved and reporting needs to be done timely. If it is purely a privacy data breach, such as an e-mail sent to the wrong address due to a typo, there is not necessarily a need for a Chief Information Security Officer whilst the other parts are still required to be involved.

32. Which of the following is most likely assigned to the Internal Audit department?
A. Data Protection Impact Assessments
B. Privacy assessments (correct)
C. Privacy Impact Assessments
D. ISO 29134
More information:
A privacy assessment can be part of an audit. However, the reason to choose option B is that the other options require decisions (not opinions) on whether sufficient (A & C) or require responsibility (D).

33. When knowing there is a process that requires an in-depth risk assessment, which of the following is least advisable?
A. A Privacy Impact Assessment
B. A Data Protection Impact Assessment
C. An express Privacy Impact Assessment (correct)
D. An organization's own Privacy Risk Assessment template
More information:
An express Privacy Impact Assessment is light, and the question already revealed that an in-depth assessment is required. Hence, option C is the correct answer. Option D reveals nothing about the depth of the assessment.

34. Which of the following contains a set of guidelines for Privacy Impact Assessments?
A. ISO 14001
B. ISO 9001
C. ISO 29134 (correct)
D. ISO 27001
More information:
Privacy Impact Assessment guidelines are contained in ISO 29134. See your study material. This is a minor detail and there is a big chance you had to guess this, which is why the question was used in this exam. There will be guessing questions on the exam. A small trick to remember is that, if you have to choose between different standards and don't know the answer, consider betting on the ISO 29xxx. Option C is the correct answer.

35. Which of the following is most important for showing compliance with the General Data Protection Regulation?
A. ISO 27001
B. Privacy Impact Assessments
C. Privacy assessments
D. Data Protection Impact Assessments (correct)
More information:
Data Protection Impact Assessments are both required by the General Data Protection Regulation in certain cases, and assess what needs to be done (or has been done) to reach the required level of protection of personal data. Hence, it shows compliance to an extent. The others do so to a lesser extent and are not mentioned in the General Data Protection Regulation.

36. What is not the goal of a security control?
A. Prevent
B. Detect
C. Administer (correct)
D. Correct
More information:
All options except for C are goals of security controls. You want to prevent an incident from happening, you want to detect an incident when it occurs so you can take action and you want to correct something when it happens. Administering is not a goal of the controls, but can be used to monitor. Option C is the correct answer.

37. What would be the most likely reason to audit a vendor?
A. To compose a processing agreement
B. To take responsibility for outsourcing (correct)
C. To solve a data breach
D. To shift responsibility
More information:
In order to outsource responsibly, an organization needs to be aware of the privacy practices of the organization it outsources to. This can be done in several ways, of which an audit is one. Option B is the correct answer, the others are less likely/realistic.

38. When designing the process of obtaining consent, which of the following is least important?
A. To verify whether an alternative legal basis can be relied on (correct)
B. To design a way to properly record it
C. To figure out where in the process to ask for consent
D. To allow for the option of reversing the consent
More information:
When already having decided consent is required, there is no need to put effort into finding an alternative legal basis. Option A is the correct answer. However, before deciding that you will ask for consent it can be fruitful to have a look at alternative legal bases, as the consent process can be cumbersome.

39. What is the best description of a processor?
A. A cloud server
B. An organization acting only as instructed by another organization (correct)
C. An organization signing a transfer agreement
D. A part-data breach responsible
More information:
Option B describes a processor, as they act as instructed by the controller. A cloud server is an example of a (possible) processor, but not a description. Option C is incorrect as this implies a separate controller. Option D is not necessarily correct, as the processor does what the controller asks.

40. What is the biggest weakness of a Data Protection Impact Assessment?
A. The Data Protection Officer has to check
B. No Chief Information Security Officer input is legally required
C. Confidentiality, Integrity and Availability are not integrated
D. It is subjective (correct)
More information:
Data Protection Impact Assessments contain a part where judgment is needed on the risks that are being posed. Which parts of the processing are risky and how risky they are is something that is difficult to determine objectively, hence due to the subjectivity the Data Protection Impact Assessment can have different outcomes when performed by different people. It is important to let a team perform the assessments, so that there is sufficient input. Option D is the correct answer.

41. Which is most true about a privacy policy?
A. Required in the European Union
B. Contains templates
C. Policies are required to be approved by the Data Protection Officer
D. Provides guidance for decisions (correct)
More information:
A policy provides guidance for an organization. Option D is the correct answer. It is not required in the European Union, it does not necessarily contain templates and there is no need for approval by the Data Protection Officer.

42. Which of the following is least likely required of an organization?
A. **Regulate (correct)**
B. Verify
C. Define
D. Confirm
More information:
An organization is not required to regulate. It can self-regulate, but this is not required. Verify, define and confirm are vague terms that can apply to anything and therefore Option A is the correct answer. Vague options like this will be part of the actual exam, so learn to reason without the vagueness affecting you.

43. After or during a data breach, what will you most likely need the marketing department for?
A. Mapping processes
B. **Sending out a mailing (correct)**
C. Investigated the breach
D. Hide the trail
More information:
When during, or after, a data breach you are required to inform the data subjects of the data breach so that they can take actions to limit possible negative consequences, you can need the marketing department because they likely have a list of all customers/clients/data subjects. Option B is the correct answer.

44. What is something communicated to people about privacy practices?
A. A mission statement
B. A privacy notice (correct)
C. A privacy strategy
D. Privacy policies and procedures
More information:
A privacy notice describes an organization's privacy practices and is communicated externally. Option B is the correct answer. Option A does not contain privacy practices, and option C and D are generally not communicated externally.

45. What is an acceptable use policy?
A. Specifies how people should behave on a network (correct)
B. A firewall setting
C. Part of the privacy program's output
D. Mandated as part of a code of ethics
More information:
See your study material. This is one of those question that asks for something that is not elaborately discussed in your study materials. There will be a few of these on the actual exam. Option A is the correct answer.

46. Who is best to sign cloud computing agreements (if available)?
A. The Chief Information Security Officer
B. The Data Protection Officer or Privacy Officer
C. The Privacy Program Manager
D. The Chief Information Officer (correct)
More information:
Your study material mentions that the Chief Information Officer should sign cloud computing agreements. If the Chief Information Officer is not an option, it should be an appropriate level of management. The Data Protection Officer is the worst option, as signing agreements could impair independence. Option D is the correct answer.

47. Which of the following would most likely be considered a data subject?
A. Any individual or natural person
B. Any legal entity
C. A person linked to data (correct)
D. A patient visiting a small shop
More information:
A person linked to data means that there is data linked to that person, meaning personal data/information, likely meaning that person is a data subject (if alive, of course). Option C is the correct answer. Option A is incomplete, as there is no mention of data. Option B is not a person. Option D also does not mention data and is incomplete.

48. If not responding quickly enough to a data subject's inquiry, which is not a likely consequence?
A. A missed legal deadline
B. A data breach (correct)
C. A complaint to the Data Protection Authority
D. A violation
More information:
The violation and the complaint are both directing at consequences of not following the law. This is done to mislead and guide the reader to doubt between the two, whereas the data breach is the correct answer as not responding to something quickly enough cannot lead to a data breach.

49. Which privacy notice is most inappropriate under the General Data Protection Regulation?
A. A one-click 20 page PDF (correct)
B. An unreadable notice due to a website being offline
C. A notice that does not fit your screen
D. A notice aimed at children, thus oversimplifying the legal basis
More information:
A 20 page PDF is likely too much to be considered simple. If there really is no way to simplify the privacy notice, consider a layered privacy notice and only deliver the information at the moment it is needed. Option A is the correct answer.

50. What is an advantage of a layered privacy notice?
A. More complete
B. Receiving relevant information only (correct)
C. Everything in one document
D. Part of a website
More information:
With a layered privacy notice, the data subject receives the relevant information only and is not confronted with a huge privacy notice of which not everything is relevant (yet). Option B is the correct answer.

51. What would be the least inappropriate use of a just-in-time notice?
A. Asking to access the location of your phone before starting your navigator (correct)
B. Asking you to write your return address on a package
C. At the time of an exam, informing you of the consequences of taking the exam
D. Your employer telling you the photos of the last company picnic are used on the company website
More information:
When you are about to use the navigator on your phone, it is appropriate to ask location access. Since it is not needed before, and can be expected to be required for a navigator, this is an appropriate just-in-time notice. Option A is the correct answer. Option B is not just-in-time, option C & D are too late.

52. What is the most likely risk when deleting data too early?
A. Having de-identified data
B. Needing to ask for consent again
C. Not complying with a legal requirement (correct)
D. Not having the right encryption
More information:
There can be legal requirements, such as financial legislation on keeping invoices, for which deleting data too early can lead to non-compliance. Option C is the correct answer.

53. Which of the following regulates the use of icons on websites and mobile screens?
A. The Data Protection Authority
B. The European Data Protection Supervisor
C. The Digital Advertising Alliance (correct)
D. The Privacy Ombudsman
More information:
The Digital Advertising Alliance self-regulates the use of icons. If you did not know this, the answer could be reasoned to due to the others options likely not being regulators. Option C is the correct answer.

54. What is the difference between express and implicit consent?
A. Opt-in versus opt-out (correct)
B. One always has a privacy notice
C. Implicit consent needs to be explicitly mentioned
D. There are no implications from express consent
More information:
Opt-in is express consent where an action needs to be taken to provide consent and opt-out is implicit consent where consent is implied unless the data subject opts out. Option A is the correct answer.

55. Of the following, which is a big reason privacy laws needed to address privacy notices?
A. They have become lengthy and complex (correct)
B. They were not in machine-readable format
C. Consent was not required before
D. Too many unsolicited mails were sent
More information:
The length and complexity was a reason people tended to skip the privacy notice, rendering it ineffective. This is part of the reason the General Data Protection Regulation requires conciseness, as well as clear and plain language. See Article 12 of the General Data Protection Regulation. Option A is the correct answer.

56. What is most important to do, if possible, when further processing personal data beyond the scope of collection?
A. Aggregate to an appropriate level (correct)
B. Use a copy in which names are removed
C. Inform data subjects
D. Update the privacy notice
More information:
Aggregating to an appropriate level implies that, if the personal data is not allowed to be processed further, the data is aggregated to a level where it is no longer personal data, or at least the unnecessary elements are removed. Option A is the correct answer. Regarding option B, even when removing the names it can still be personal data, especially if there is a copy which still includes the names.

57. When sending e-mails to data subjects, what can most likely cause an issue?
A. Mailbox size limitations
B. Cost of storage
C. A copy in the sent folder
D. Improper encryption (correct)
More information:
If the message is not properly encrypted and is intercepted, the intercepting party can read it. How realistic/likely this is can be debated, but of the options provided it is the only issue related to possible unintended disclosure. Option D is the correct answer.

58. When setting up an automated mailing system, which is likely most important?
A. Delivering the privacy notice with the e-mail
B. Asking an opt-in prior to every e-mail
C. Proper retention periods of the e-mail
D. Ensuring the commercial message is not unsolicited (correct)
More information:
Unsolicited messages are never a good idea, as they could result in unlawful processing or violations of regulations (such as CAN-SPAM). Option D is the correct answer.

59. Which US state was the first to require a conspicuously posted privacy notice?
A. Delaware
B. California (correct)
C. New York
D. Minnesota
More information:
The California Online Privacy Protection Act was the first to require a conspicuously posted privacy notice, hence option B is the correct answer.

60. What is important to do before providing someone access to their data?
A. Setting up a retention scheme
B. Determining the legal basis
C. Seeing whether it fits the organizational workload
D. Verifying their identity (correct)
More information:
Verifying someone's identity is necessary and required by some laws. If data is provided to the wrong person, this is potentially a data breach. Option D is the correct answer.

61. What will companies in the public eye relying on data most likely realize at some point?
A. A privacy program is required
B. Customer trust is needed (correct)
C. International data transfers are not necessary
D. Only with a privacy program can the company implement best practices
More information:
When an organization relies on data, it is important that the customers whose data the organization relies on trust the organization with their data. Hence, option B is the correct answer. A privacy program can be useful but no law requires it (yet), whether international data transfers are necessary is not necessarily relevant because they are not necessarily unsafe, and best practices can also be implemented without a privacy program.

62. When someone wants his/her data corrected, what is the most likely point to pay attention to?
A. The organizational workload
B. The backlog of rectifications
C. Checking the new data for accuracy
D. The connection of data elements and locations (correct)
More information:
When something is changed in one location, an organization has to make sure it is also changed on all other locations that use (part of) the same data. Option D is the correct answer. Option A and B are no excuse, and option C is true to some extent but less important than option D.

63. Why is it important to recognize an Article 15 General Data Protection Regulation request when someone sends a complaint to your organization?
A. Because of reputational damage
B. To remain having a legal basis for processing
C. Because of the legal deadline (correct)
D. To prevent a data breach
More information:
There is no standard format for an Article 15 access request, so it can be hidden in a complaint. If an Article 15 request is sent, where a data subject asks for a copy of his/her personal data, there is a legal deadline. Option C is the correct answer. Option A could also be a consequence, but a consequence of missing the deadline. Option B and D are irrelevant.

64. In the case of the data breach at Uber in 2016, how did Uber attempt to solve the situation?
A. Pay hackers (correct)
B. Increase security
C. Hire private investigators
D. Litigate
More information:
Uber tried to solve the issue by paying the hackers. This was in your study material. Pay attention to other cases in your study material, as the exam can contain questions concerning these cases. Option A is the correct answer.

Use this scenario for the following three questions:

An internet reseller buys up cheap products and sells them for a slightly higher price. The company has a high turnover, and business is going well. There are only three employees working for the company, which is all that is needed as most is automatically shipped from a third party warehouse, with an online order that triggers an automated process.

Since the company is small, it does not standardize its work practices. Each employee has its own way of getting things done, and if needed they will ask the boss, who is generally in the same office and happy to assist.

One day, the server where all orders are stored is without password protection due to an accidental password reset. The cloud provider calls the company's boss to ask why they performed the reset, and after finding out that it was an accident, offers to check whether any external party has accessed the company's data in the hours it was freely accessible. This offer is refused, as the boss of the company regards the data not to be sensitive, as it only concerns customer orders.

65. In the scenario provided, where is the organization on the Privacy Maturity Model?
A. Ad hoc (correct)
B. Managed
C. Defined
D. Optimized
More information:
That the organization does not have standardized work practices indicates that the organization is at the Ad hoc level.

66. What should the company have done in light of the password reset?
A. No data breach took place, since accessing it would have been illegal, so no action is needed
B. The cloud provider is responsible in case of a data breach, so no action is needed
C. The company should have accepted the offer in order to determine whether a data breach took place (correct)
D. If a data processing agreement is in place, no action is needed
More information:
After a possible data breach, it is very important to determine whether a data breach actually took place. If data has been accessed by external parties, certain regulations would require the organization to inform the data subjects or report the data breach to a supervisory authority. Option C is the correct answer.

67. What would have been the case if an external person accessed the data?
A. It would have required immediate contact with the Data Protection Authority
B. It would likely have been a data breach (correct)
C. If the persons that accessed the data do not spread it, there is no issue
D. An audit should have been performed
More information:
If external parties accessed the data, and personal data was part of that, it would have been a data breach in the context of certain privacy laws. The size and impact of the data breach would then have to be determined, as this influences whether the breach would be reportable or has to be communicated to the data subjects. Option B is the correct answer.

68. Which of the following is a likely consequence of not knowing how and what you are processing?
A. Avoid liability of mishandling
B. Risk avoidance
C. Unaware of consequences of mishandling (correct)
D. Increase risk appetite
More information:
If you do not know what data you are processing, you cannot make a reliable estimate of what the consequences are in case a data breach occurs or the data is used incorrectly. Option C is the correct answer. Option D can be argued to be true, but if C is one step before D and therefore the correct option.

69. Development of your privacy awareness program can most likely be shared with which of the following?
A. The ethics and integrity department (correct)
B. The legal department
C. The management board
D. The audit department
More information:
The ethics and integrity department in an organization generally attempts to raise awareness, through training and campaigns. They could prove to be helpful for raising awareness for the privacy practices. The other departments are less likely to be involved in raising awareness. Option A is the correct answer.

70. Why do Chief Executive Officers not always give priority to privacy program implementation?
A. There is no risk of a fine
B. A secure cloud server is used in modern organizations
C. It does not generate revenue (correct)
D. The organization is small
More information:
Privacy costs money and does not generate revenue and management is generally only interested because they are legally required to be, not because they see the importance (which will hopefully change). A privacy incident or loss of consumer trust, however, can cost a lot more than proper privacy practices. Option C is the correct answer.

71. Which of the following is the least common way to describe data about someone?
A. Private data (correct)
B. Personal data
C. Personal information
D. Personally identifiable information
More information:
Private data is the least common term used amongst the options provided. Option A is the correct answer. There will be a few easy questions like this on the exam. Try to briefly check if they really are as easy as they appear, because questions on the exam are often phrased to trick the test taker into choosing the incorrect answer.

72. Where was Privacy by Design most likely developed?
A. The European Union
B. The United States
C. The United Kingdom
D. Canada (correct)
More information:
Former Information and Privacy Commissioner for Ontario, Canada, Ann Cavoukian came up with the concept of privacy by design. Option D is the correct answer. This is a useless fact, but there will likely be useless facts asked during the exam.

73. A mobile phone application that will not function without an "unnecessary" connection to the internet at some point, is most likely not following which of the Privacy by Design principles?
A. Proactive, not reactive
B. Visibility and transparency
C. End-to-end security (correct)
D. Privacy as default
More information:
From start to finish there should be strong security measures. An unnecessary connection weakens security, and hence this principle is not respected. Option C is the correct answer. Option A and B cannot be concluded on with the amount of information in the question. Option D could also be correct, but in this case there is not even an option for privacy, so D is not the correct answer.

74. Which of the following is not Privacy by Design?
A. Being proactive
B. Embedded privacy controls
C. Demonstrating respect for users
D. Being reactive (correct)
More information:
Being reactive is the opposite of by design. Option D is the correct answer.

75. When during the design of a process you consider making use of a third-party, which would be most exemplary of Privacy by Design?
A. Determining whether a third-party is needed (correct)
B. Using a well written contract
C. Ensuring only processors in safe countries are contracted
D. Involving the third party in the design
More information:
Privacy by Design entails taking the fewest privacy risks possible. If the use of a third-party can be avoided, it is generally better to do so (unless the third-party actually increases security). Of all the options provided, option A is the best.

76. When password protection is too strict, which of the following is most likely negatively impacted?
A. Encryption
B. DDOS attacks
C. Availability (correct)
D. Integrity
More information:
When the encryption is too heavy, and it takes too much time to decrypt, or the encryption is too sensitive to damages (such as an old fashioned hard drives with damages, rendering decryption difficult/impossible), the data is less available. Option C is the correct answer.

77. If you are looking for guidance on the security management system implementation, which would you look?
A. ISO/IEC 2700
B. ISO 9001
C. ISO 14001
D. ISO/IEC 27003 (correct)
More information:
A very specific question, but ISO/IEC 27003 contains information security management system implementation guidance. Option D is the correct answer. Some questions will be specific. If you know the answer that is great, but there is room for mistakes so do not worry too much when missing a question. Just flag it and come back to it at the end.

78. When implementing a privacy program, what is important regarding access to files?
A. The Chief Information Security Officer should have access to all files
B. The Chief Information Security Officer determines who has access
C. Roles should determine access (correct)
D. Access is linked to individuals
More information:
Access should be linked to roles. This, for example, prevents someone who changes roles in an organization to still have access that is not needed in the new role. Option C is the correct answer.

79. Where would you most likely not find guidance on data breach reporting in the United States?
A. Comprehensive federal privacy law (correct)
B. State law
C. Industry-specific federal law
D. The General Data Protection Regulation
More information:
There is, at the moment, no comprehensive federal privacy law in the United States. This should be obvious from your study material. Hence, it cannot be a source of guidance for data breach reporting. Option A is the correct answer.

80. What would most likely help you get executives on your side regarding data breach prevention?
A. Showing the monetary impact of a data breach (correct)
B. Taking the General Data Protection Regulation as an example
C. Planning a meeting involving the Chief Information Security Officer
D. Indicating the statistical likelihood
More information:
When management sees how much non-compliance can cost, they will likely weigh that against the cost of compliance. If non-compliance likely costs a lot more, the resources for compliance will more likely be freed up. Option A is the correct answer. Option D also helps, but not without showing the monetary impact.

81. Which of the following is the most common cause of a data breach?
A. System glitches
B. Failing firewalls
C. Simple encryption
D. Malicious actors (correct)
More information:
See your study materials, malicious actors are the most common cause of a data breach of the options presented. Option D is the correct answer.

82. What is an informal readiness testing activity?
A. A policy evaluation
B. An incident response planning
C. Scenario testing
D. A tabletop exercise (correct)
More information:
A tabletop exercise is a structured yet informal desk exercise to test the readiness of an organization and see how all roles and responsibilities result in solving a certain (emergency) situation. Option D is the correct answer. Option A and C sound correct, but are not the terms used in your study material. Option B is planning, not testing.

83. What is likely the most important goal of metrics for an organization?
A. Legal compliance
B. Count data breaches
C. Inform the organization (correct)
D. Deter hackers
More information:
Metrics provide information by quantifying a situation, hence they inform the organization. Option C is the correct answer.

Use this scenario for the following three questions:

A clinic has just hired you as a privacy program manager. The clinic specializes in surgeries that reverse decisions taken by parents, such as circumcision, which patients wish to reverse due to disagreement with the decisions their parents took regarding their child's body. Your team consists of the privacy officer, which is close to the age of retirement and has been assigned the privacy officer job because nobody else wanted to do it, and the security officer who will start the same day as you.

On your first day you familiarize yourself with the staff and the procedures that are in place. You do so in an effort to determine the best approach towards compliance and optimal privacy practices. The task proves somewhat difficult, as it seems every doctor in the clinic maintains different procedures. The procedures are written down though, so that helps, but there is no data on compliance with the policies.

Besides the need to identify how the current situation needs to be changed in order to be compliant with the privacy legislation, the management board has purchased software that automatically sends data about the patients' treatment to their health insurance provider, saving the administrative staff a lot of work.

84. In the provided scenario, where is the organization on the Privacy Maturity Model?
A. Ad hoc
B. Managed
C. Optimized
D. Repeatable (correct)
More information:
Since the organization has procedures in place for all practices, albeit different ones for every doctor, the level is Repeatable. Ad hoc would be the correct answer if there were incomplete and inconsistent procedures, which does not seem to be the case here. Managed and optimized would require the effectiveness having been assessed, which is not the case here.

85. If a patient named Achmet comes in for a reverse-circumcision, which of the following elements would least likely be considered sensitive personal data in the European Union?
A. Bank account and insurance number (correct)
B. The likelihood of a certain religion
C. The information of a venereal disease
D. Any complications after the surgery
More information:
Bank account and insurance number are not considered sensitive personal data under the General Data Protection Regulation, however important they may be under other legislation. Option A is the correct answer. Anything regarding someone's religion, including likelihood, is sensitive personal data. Any medical information, such as venereal diseases or complications, are sensitive personal data.

86. Since it is unclear whether the procedures that are already in place are effective and/or followed, what is the best approach to find out?
A. Management evaluation
B. The verdict of the Chief Information Security Officer
C. The use of metrics (correct)
D. Composing Binding Corporate Rules
More information:
If policies and procedures are in place, there are likely measurable aspects to these policies and expected outcomes. With the use of metrics the effectiveness of the policies can be measured. Option C is the correct answer. Option A may result in a biased review as management wants as few problems as possible, and option B will also result in a biased review since the Chief Information Security Officer will never think things are secure enough. Option D just entails creating more procedures.

87. What could be a possible advantage of implementing a market leader's privacy metrics software as opposed to your own?
A. Automatic registration
B. High security
C. Benchmarking (correct)
D. Lower likelihood of a data breach
More information:
A market leader likely has an option to share performance with other customers, in an effort to benchmark. This way you can see how your organization performs compared to other organizations. Option C is the correct answer. Option A and B are also possible creating your own software.

88. What right is granted under the Federal Credit Reporting Act?
A. The right to be forgotten
B. No adverse decisions to be made
C. Blocking credit reports from being used
D. Access to all information a consumer reporting agency has on them (correct)
More information:
See your study material on the Federal Credit Reporting Act. Option D is the correct answer.

89. To whom/what should the Data Protection Officer report in an organization in the European Union?
A. The Chief Information Security Officer
B. The Chief Financial Officer
C. The Chief Information Officer
D. The Chief Executive Officer (correct)
More information:
The Data Protection Officer should report to the highest level of management possible. From the options provided, that is the Chief Executive Officer, hence option D is the correct answer.

90. What is a regular, ad hoc or on demand process of checking control elements?
A. Control testing
B. An audit (correct)
C. A firewall test run
D. Privacy metrics
More information:
An audit is a regular, ad hoc or on demand process of checking control elements. Option B is the correct answer. The audit department can do more, and can even provide consulting services, but for this question it fits option B best.

Printed in Poland
by Amazon Fulfillment
Poland Sp. z o.o., Wrocław